BACKART

On the Flip Side

Have fun with the back too!

Eddie Leore

Danita Rafalovich and Kathryn Alison Pellman

Cover Quilt: Detail of "High Voltage" by Liz Axford (the full piece is shown on
pages 30 and 31) Photo: Jack Mathieson

Photographic credits:
Stephen Attig; *page 61*
Liz Axford; *page 48*
Sue Benner; *pages 16, 18 and 19*
Brian Blauser; *pages 44 and 45*
Ken Burris; *pages 6 and 7*
John Carlano; *page 4*
Geoffrey Carr; *pages 8 and 9*
Colortek; *pages 34, 35, 43, 75 and 80*
Caryl Bryer Fallert; *pages 32, 33, 58 and 59*
Jerry De Felice; *page 39*
Patty Hawkins; *page 27*
Judy Hopkins; *page 15*
Jack Mathieson; *pages 3, 11, 12, 13, 14, 17, 22, 23, 24, 25, 30, 31, 37, 38,
    40, 41, 42, 49, 50, 51, 52, 53, 54, 55, 56, 57, 60, 62, 63, 64, 65, 68,
    69, 73, 74 and 79*
Tom Moulin; *pages 10 and 36*
Sharon Reisdorph; *pages 20, 21, 26, 28, 29, 30 and 31*
Wayne Smith, *page 79*
Eileen Sullivan; *pages 46 and 47*
Rozemaryn van der Horst; *pages 66 and 67*
Judi Warren; *page 71*
Susan Galloway Wilson; *page 70*

The artists retain copyright to the individual works shown in this book.

Published by: Leone Publications
              2628 Bayshore Drive
              Mt. View, California, U.S.A. 94043

Design and Production: Terri Wanke

Printed in Hong Kong

ISBN No. 0-942786-10-6
10 9 8 7 6 5 4 3 2

Contents

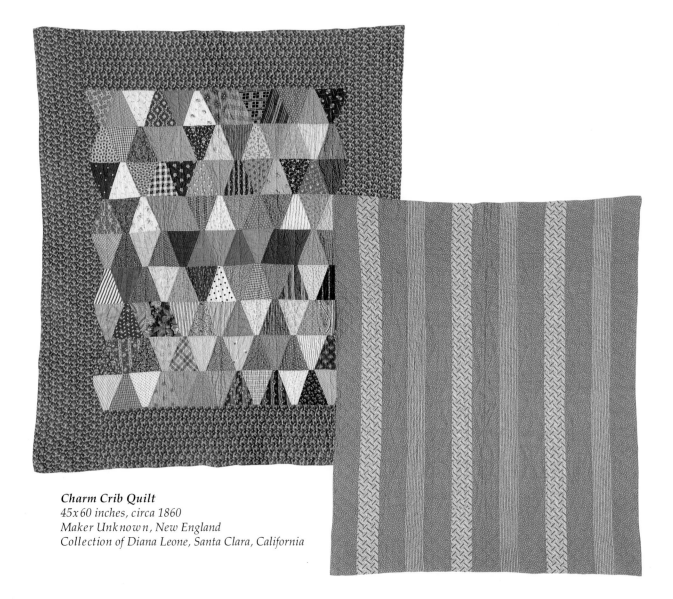

Charm Crib Quilt
45x60 inches, circa 1860
Maker Unknown, New England
Collection of Diana Leone, Santa Clara, California

Acknowledgments

We want to thank all the quilters who shared their quilts with us, especially the quilters whose work appears in this book. Your generous contributions have made this book possible. Also, special appreciation goes to all our family and friends for their encouragement and support.

Postage Stamp Quilt (detail of back)
72 x 72 inches, 1990
Kathleen W. Francis, Robin L. Smith and
Friends, Pennsylvania

Introduction

Backart is a word we coined in 1987 when writing our first article. The terms *two-sided quilt* and *pieced back* did not express the feelings we had about our quilt backs and what we were experiencing while making them. We wanted to express the idea of using the empty back of the quilt as a canvas.

For quiltmakers, backart encourages freedom of expression going beyond the structured rules often confronting them when designing the front. Backart provides an opportunity to take chances and experiment with new ideas, allowing room for creativity and growth.

One of the questions we are frequently asked is, "What made you decide to do something different with the quilt back?"

Danita's first pieced back was created when she used blocks left over from the front and arranged them into a center medallion. Kathryn made her first pieced back when she found that she had not purchased enough of one fabric to fill the back. She combined the fabric with pieces left over from the front and created a diagonal back.

Another question often asked is, "What style of quilts can have backart?"

Our response is, "All quilts." Many quilters who make pieced backs work with innovative rather than traditional quilt patterns. We have tried to present a broad representation of quilting styles to inspire every quilter, regardless of personal style or technical ability.

There are no right or wrong answers to backart, only what works best for you.

We have arranged the quilts into chapters, presenting them according to the backart technique used. The exception to this is the first group of quilts; they are from the past and show that backart is new in name only. The final chapter, "Backart Techniques," provides the basic steps needed to create a pieced back.

Backart from the Past

Many examples of historical quilts with pieced backs document that backart had early beginnings. Occasionally, backs were made by alternating red and green pieced columns averaging ten inches in width. Some of the earlier pieced backs were produced by the Mennonites, a Protestant sect from Pennsylvania noted for plain and simple living. Backart can also be found on quilts from Missouri and Alabama. Myron and Patsy Orlofsky comment in their book, *Quilts in America*, that pieced backs "...may have been a rural Southern tradition."

Centennial Quilt
89 x 94 inches, Late Nineteenth Century
Maker Unknown
Collection of Shelburne Museum, Shelburne, Vermont

This quilt, made from patriotic and centennial fabrics, was
originally meant for a four poster bed. Two squares, making up
the bottom corners, were added later. The back is composed of
a number of handkerchiefs. The center handkerchief honors the
1876 Centennial Exhibition at Fairmont Park in Philadelphia; one
handkerchief is from the 1893 Chicago World's Fair; another
contains the wording of The Declaration of Independence.

Variable Star and Nine Patch
50 x 50 inches, circa 1856
Maker Unknown, Lowell, Massachusetts
Collection of Rowland and Eleanor Miller, Louisville, Kentucky

On the back of this crib quilt called "Walk Around," the name, Alfred P. Sawyer, and his birth date, August 20, 1856, are written on a patch in the center.

Antique Sampler
80 x 80 inches, circa 1856
Maker Unknown, Pennsylvania
Collection of Diana Leone, Santa Clara, California

Occasionally two quilt tops were united as one. This double sampler was carefully planned so that the front and back seams align.

10

Star and Pigpen
58 x 74 inches, circa 1940
Katherine Summerville, Aliceville, Alabama
Collection of Robert Cargo Folk Art Gallery, Tuscaloosa, Alabama

This inspirational African-American quilt reflects the total abandon of traditional quilting. The curved quilting lines contrast beautifully with the horizontal/vertical pieced back.

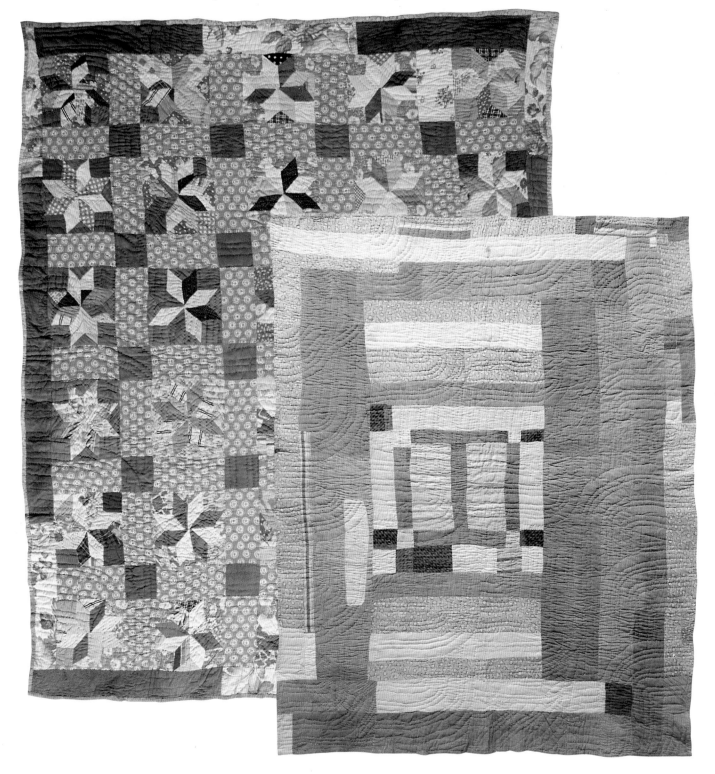

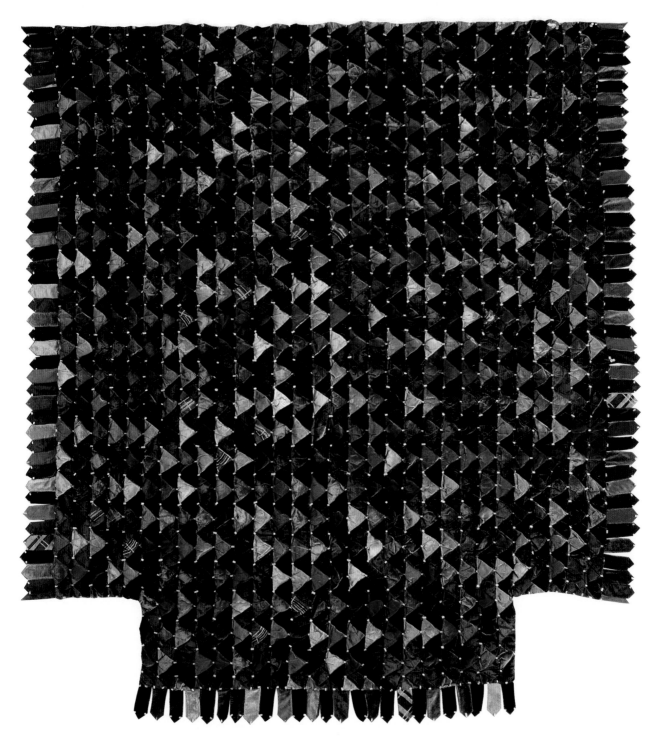

Victorian Crazy Quilt
76 x 87 inches, circa 1900
Maker Unknown, Peoria, Illinois
Collection of Cheryl Trostrud-White, Calabasas, California

The maker of this unusual double-sided quilt worked in a
coffin factory and used scraps of velvets to create the quilt's
colorful design. Velvet strips with pointed ends form the
free-hanging picket fence border on three sides.

Fabric Grids

Lengths of fabric are sewn together into columns or rows with the
longest seams running either horizontally, vertically, or in both
directions, creating a grid-like pattern.

Japanese Yukata
79 x 80 inches, 1990
Danita Rafalovich, Los Angeles, California

Yukata is a lightweight cotton robe worn in Japan after
taking a hot bath or in the summer months when the
weather is hot and humid. Traditional 14 inch yukata fabrics
create the robe on the front and compose the back.

Lagnaippe
41.5 x 51 inches, 1987
Terri Shinn, Anchorage, Alaska

Lagnaippe is Cajun for "a little something extra." In this case, the something extra is hand-sewn watermelon seeds, 200 buttons, snaps and a border made from scraps of fabric. Three pieced panels of antique quilt blocks and old flour sacks make up the back. "Backs offer more freedom than the front," says the maker, "and I have no idea how they will turn out."

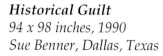

Historical Guilt
94 x 98 inches, 1990
Sue Benner, Dallas, Texas

This quilt represents a pondering of
racial issues and their history in our
country. The overall design contains
several symbolic images, including a
curtain, gate, threshold and barrier.

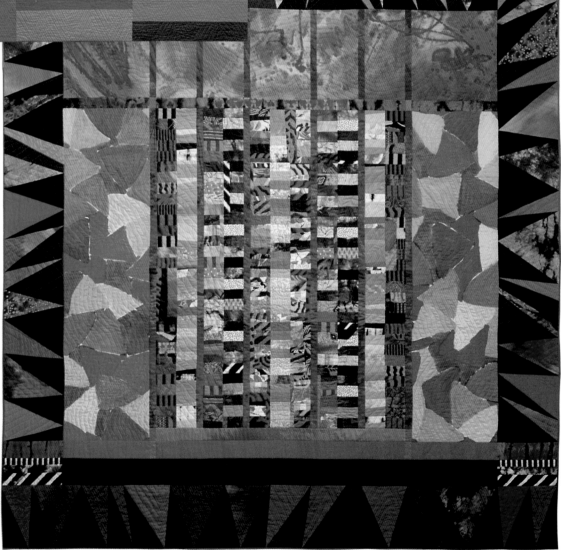

Hawaiian Houses
58 x 63 inches, 1987
Susan Milstein, Los Angeles, California

Colorful houses made from Hawaiian cottons fill the front of
this quilt. On the back, the maker exhibited her extensive
collection of tropical fabrics in two pieced columns sewn to
the sides of 43" wide fabric.

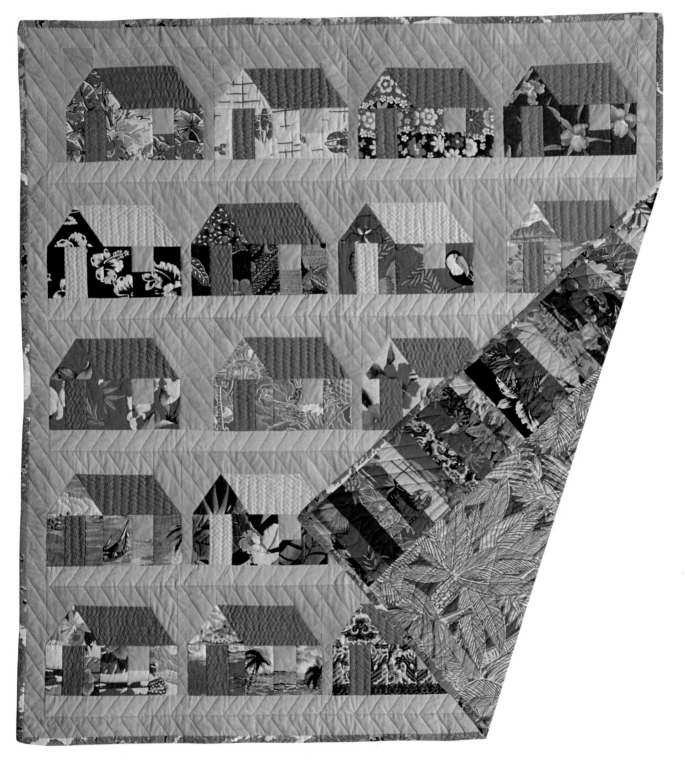

Expectations 1: A Cold, Cloudy Day
73 x 73 inches, 1990
Sue Benner, Dallas, Texas

This quilt is the first in a series of two-sided quilts expressing
the maker's feelings while contemplating motherhood. The
back illustrates the winter day she and her husband decided
to start their family.

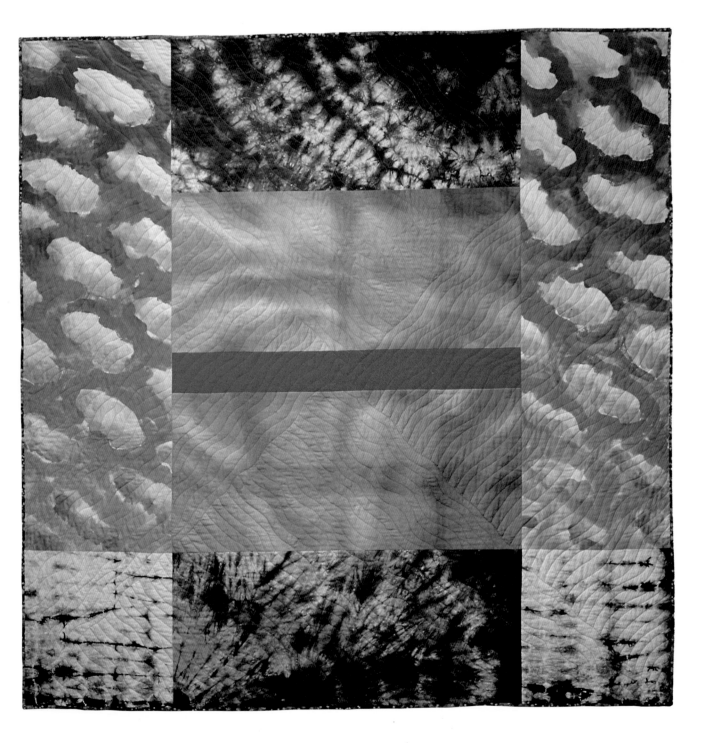

This Is a Long Distance Call
56 x 53 inches, 1987
Yvonne Porcella, Modesto, California

Large pieces of Japanese pictorial fabric on both sides tell the
story of a Samurai warrior on a long distance call to a Geisha
girl. The miniature baby dolls on the back tell the happy
ending. The checkerboard tubular sleeve allows either side
to be the front.

Backs on a Slant

A diagonal cut is useful when the selected back fabric is too short to fit the back in either direction. Fabric is cut at an angle and sewn so that the primary seam is on a slant — not parallel to any side of the quilt.

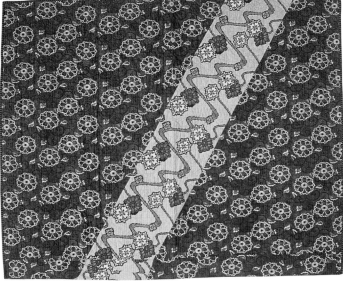

Japanese Sampler
60 x 76 inches, 1991
Danita Rafalovich, Los Angeles, California

Old and antique Japanese fabrics compose the front. The back utilizes the simplest diagonal cut with 14 inch wide *yukata* fabric filling the space.

Plaid Compass Rose
96 x 96 inches, 1989
Judy Mathieson, Woodland Hills, California

The diagonal strips on the back echo the diagonal set on the front of this traditional quilt. The bottom left star on the back (detailed below) is over 100 years old.

Slower Traffic Keep Right
48 x 64 inches, 1989
Danita Rafalovich, Los Angeles, California

This quilt celebrates life and our busy schedules. The round, central rubber stamped area represents a traffic circle where we find ourselves going around and around. The back, constructed with pieces left over from the front, incorporates the horizontal/ vertical technique and a variation of the diagonal technique.

25

Year of the Dragon
86 x 66 inches, 1988
Kathryn Alison Pellman, Los Angeles, California

Bas relief dragons on the temple walls of northern Thailand inspired this quilt. The traditional clam shell pattern appliqued to the Thai silk background makes the dragon's scales. The sun motif, too bold for the front, was placed along the diagonal pieced strip on the back.

5.5 On the Richter Scale
66 x 81 inches, 1989
Patty Hawkins, Lyons, Colorado

In this quilt, influenced by earth-
quakes, red triangular sections
look like splitting watermelons.
The fracture in the lower right
hand corner of the back continues
the theme.

Moonlight Serenade
66 x 45 inches, 1989
Kathryn Alison Pellman, Los Angeles, California

The coyotes are made with Seminole patchwork. Leftover
fabrics are sewn together to form the colorful diagonal on
the back. The pieced sleeve completes the design.

At the Hop
96 x 76 inches, 1988
Kathryn Alison Pellman, Los Angeles, California

This contemporary view of a fifties dance features couples
framed in circles representing spotlights or phonograph
records. The preprinted fabric label in the center of the back
was found after the quilt was named.

High Voltage
52 x 50 inches, 1988
Liz Axford, Houston, Texas

Geometric shapes of pure, bold colors on the back are
created by using a variation of the diagonal cut. The tilted
"T" gives the quilt a feeling of movement. The maker uses
the back "as a quick design exercise, and as a way to use
pieces left over from the front."

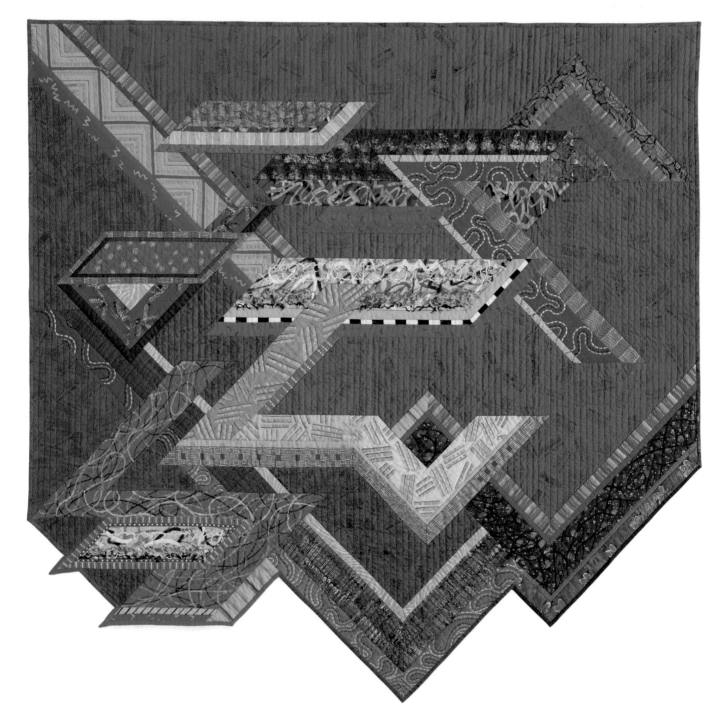

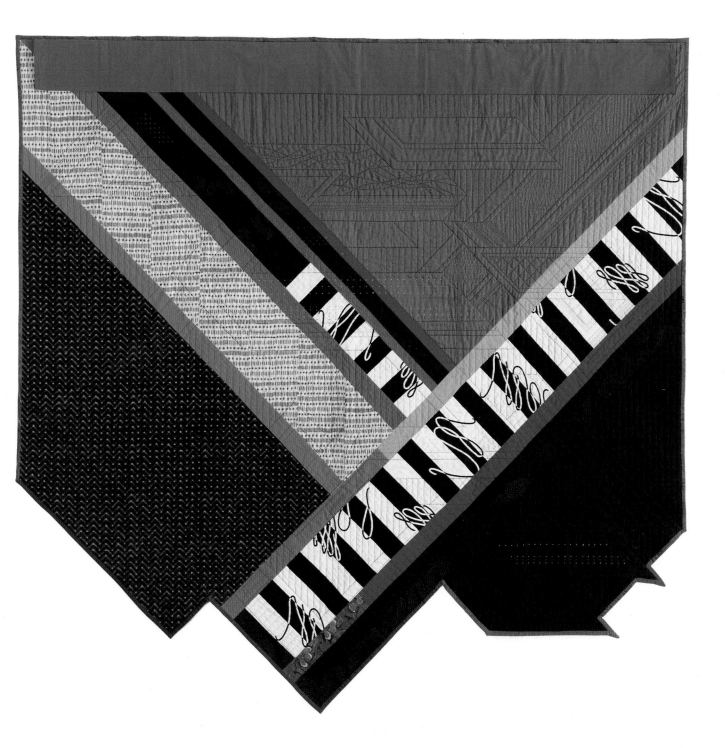

31

Framing Possibilities

Serving the same purpose as a picture frame, the fabric frame focuses
the viewer's eye on a special fabric. Multiple frames, similar to
multiple mats around artwork, can creatively be used to further
enhance the central design.

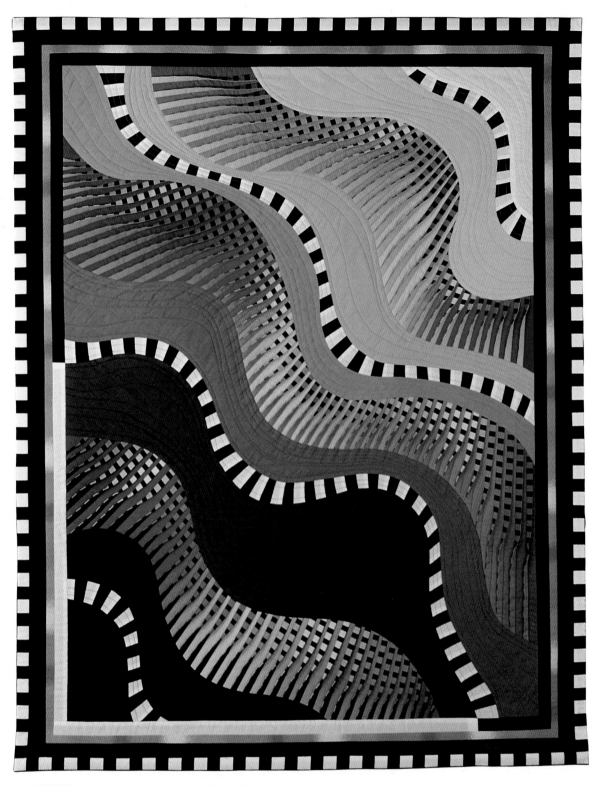

Chromatic Progressions #2
43 x 54 inches, 1991
Caryl Bryer Fallert, Oswego, Illinois

In music, *chromatic* means "progressing by half tones." It
also means "having color." The word's interpretation is seen
in the waves of changing colors undulating across the front.
A log cabin, made from leftover dyed fabrics, progresses by
frames to fill the back.

Framing the Ridiculous
46 x 52 inches, 1989
Danita Rafalovich, Los Angeles, California

This quilt is the result of a theme challenge, "Bordering on the Absurd." Irregularly shaped squares on the back occasionally fall out of their frame, floating freely. The front and back have rubber stamp art. A stamped label completes the back's design.

Monet's Water Lilies
42 x 42 inches, 1989
Diana Leone, Santa Clara, California

This log cabin impressionistic interpretation was made prior to viewing an exhibit of Monet's work. The framed silk scarf, depicting the painting by Monet, was found after the front was made.

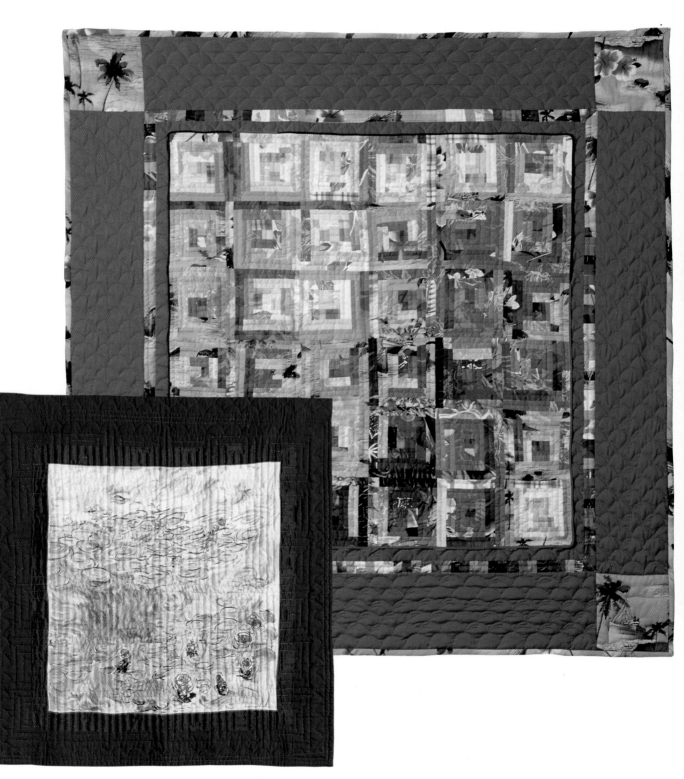

Six x Six Comes Up Roses
87 x 101 inches, 1990
Kathleen H. McCrady, Austin, Texas

The center of this quilt was inspired by
a pieced quilt from the 1800s. The
challenge was in the drafting and
piecing of the intricate six-pointed
stars. Broderie perse is used on the
front and appears again on the back in
one of the multiple frames.

It's a Wonderful Life
54 x 66 inches, 1989
Danita Rafalovich, Los Angeles, California

Views of life from a different perspective are rubber stamped in
the attic windows. Four framed scenes on the back surround
the quilt's label containing the subtitle "Rubber Stamp Quilt."

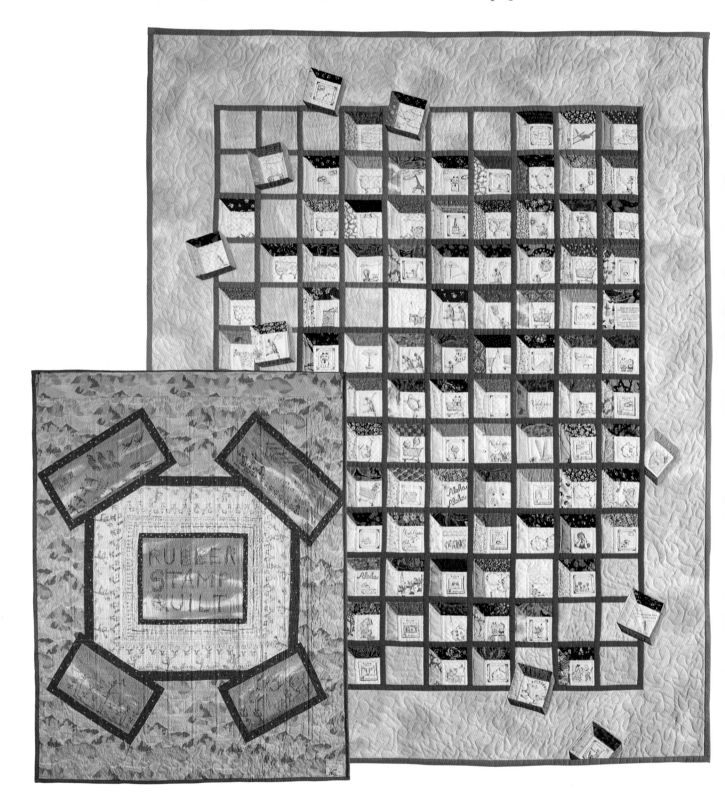

Winchester Charm
99 x 106 inches, 1989
Marie Goyette Fritz, San Diego, California

The Winchester Mystery House in San Jose, California, was
under continual construction during its owner's lifetime.
Named after the house, this quilt is also never-ending. Each
year, three floating blocks (nine new fabrics) are added to
the back. As of January 1991, the quilt, all hand pieced,
contained 2,829 different fabrics.

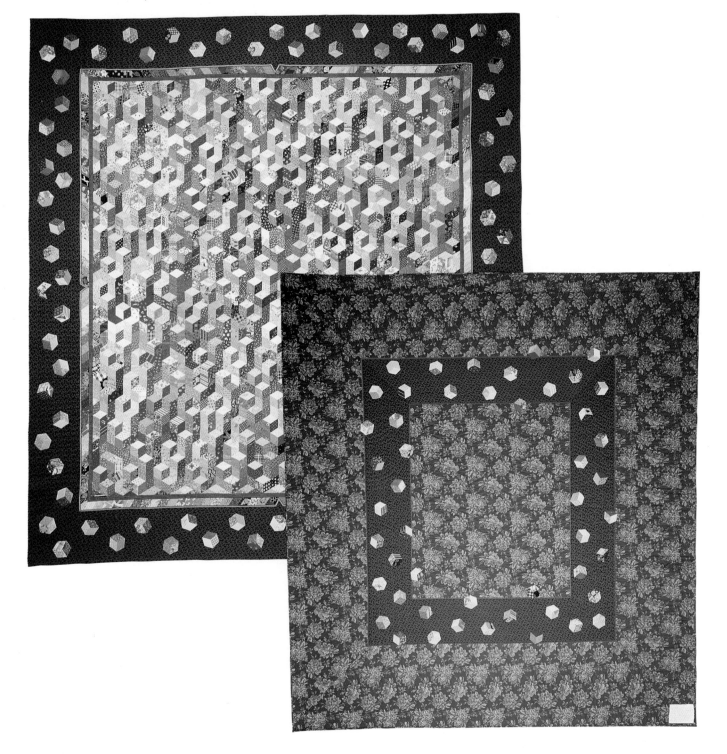

Herd of Cats
35 x 50 inches, 1990
Kathryn Alison Pellman, Los Angeles, California

"It's like trying to lead a herd of cats," was the remark of a
Los Angeles City Councilman in reference to his fellow
council members. Inspired by this statement, the maker
created fifteen cats surrounding City Hall. On the back, a
cat wears a T-shirt with the quote.

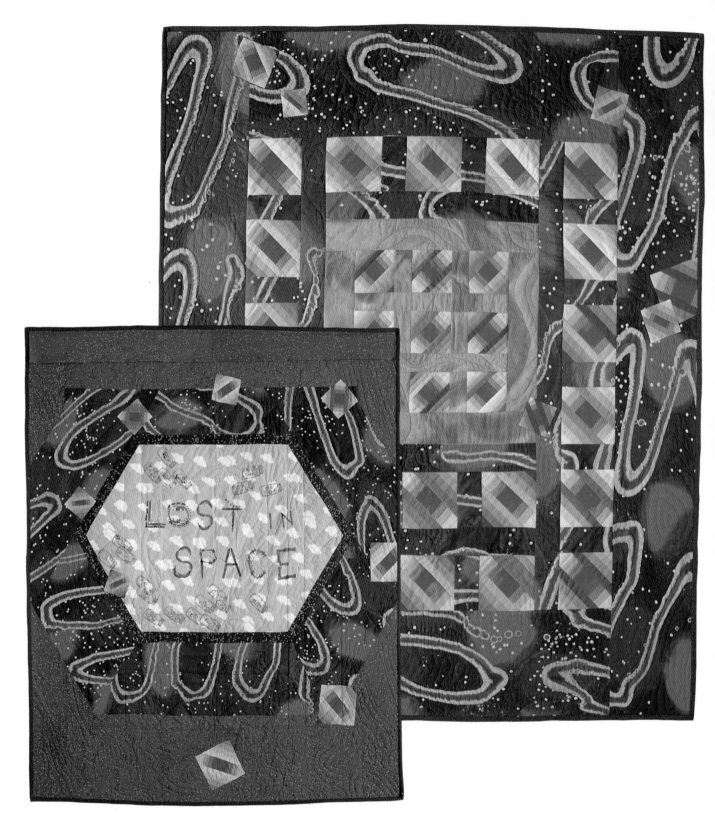

Lost in Space
54 x 66 inches, 1989
Danita Rafalovich, Los Angeles, California

Blocks made from hand-dyed fabrics appear to be floating in
space on both sides of this quilt. They begin to break from
the orderly pattern on the front. On the back, they swirl
around the rubber stamped label.

Untitled Dog
17 x 9-1/2 inches, 1991
Kathryn Alison Pellman, Los Angeles, California
Collection of Ellen Pressman and Jeffery Tohl, Studio City, California

Japanese fabrics used on the front and on the multi-framed back remind the owners of their honeymoon in Japan.

43

A Nuestra Señora La Virgen de Guadalupe
77 x 76 inches, 1991
Beth Thomas Kennedy, Austin, Texas

A fascinating array of Mexican artifacts combine with cottons, blends and oilcloth to celebrate the Virgin of Guadalupe and the colors and culture of the Mexican people. A variety of items left over from the front are incorporated into the back.

Design Elements

A design element is often incorporated into a quilt's border to provide unity. It can also be used on the back to unify the quilt's two surfaces.

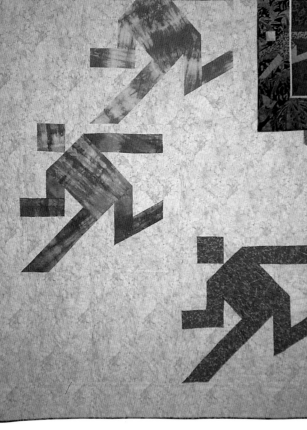

Warning: Some Colors May Run
63 x 76 inches, 1991
Judith Reilly, Brookfield, Connecticut

A simplified version of the design element appears on the back.

Lake Arrowhead Houses
43 x 43 inches, 1987
Carol Rhodes, Sunset Beach, California

House blocks are repeated in this
African-American stylized quilt. The
design element on the front is enlarged
on the back.

Waiting on the Thunder
39 x 51 inches, 1989
Liz Axford, Houston, Texas

This quilt takes its name from a passage in the Bob Seger song, "Night Moves." The juxtaposition of light and dark triangles creates the streak of lightning pattern.

Designer Triangles - Painted Amish
56 x 56 inches, 1988
Kathleen H. McCrady, Austin, Texas

The back is an enlarged design element from the front.
Large pieces of solid fabric showcase the fine hand quilting.

Grandmother's Road to California: The Life of a Mennonite Woman
40 x 75 inches, 1989
Trudy Bergen,
Los Angeles, California
Collection of
Harry L. Bergen,
Bakersfield, California

Major events in the life of
the maker's grandmother
are represented by the
blocks on the front. The
central design element —
the cross — repeats on the
back aligning exactly with
the front cross. The back is
one large label, a written
history of her grand-
mother's life.

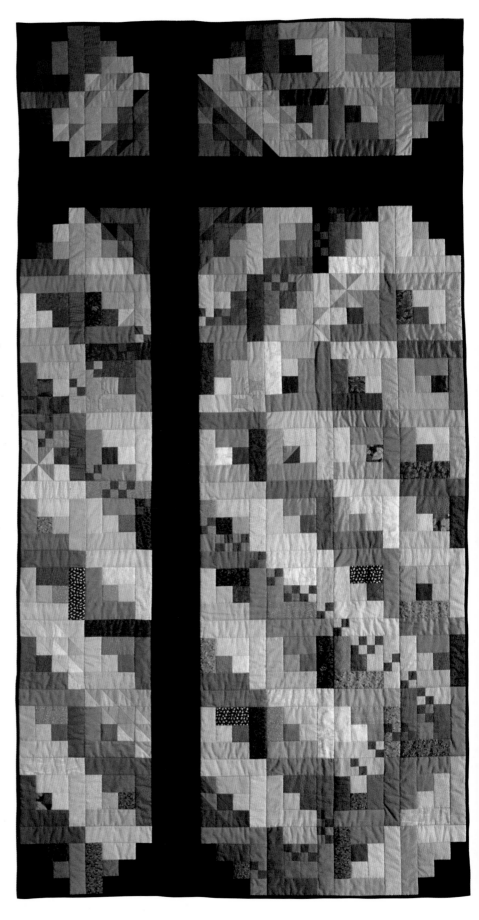

50

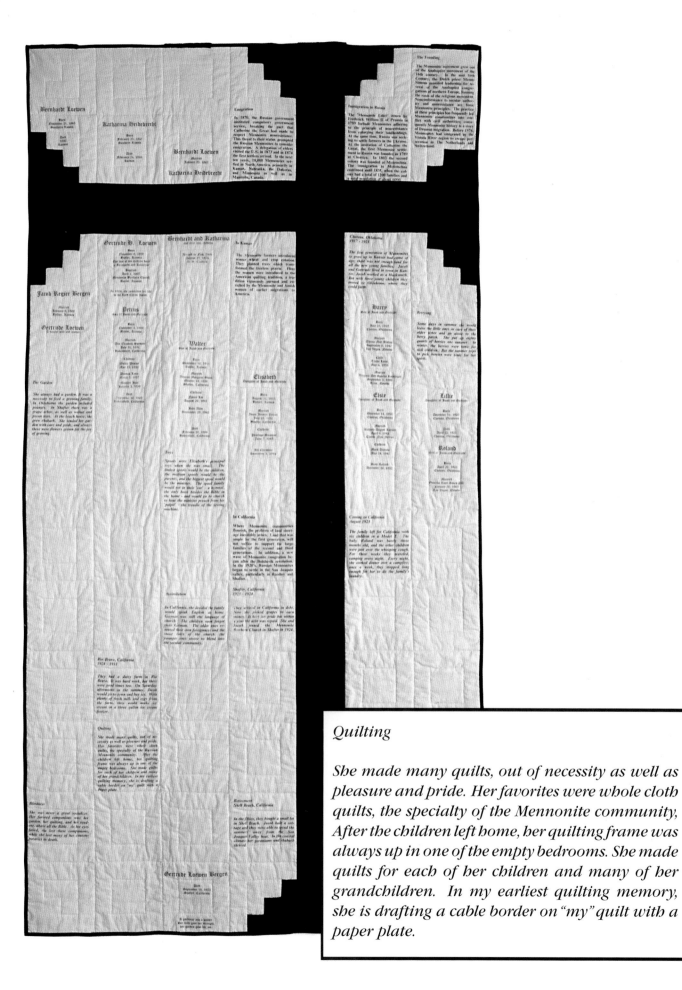

Quilting

She made many quilts, out of necessity as well as pleasure and pride. Her favorites were whole cloth quilts, the specialty of the Mennonite community, After the children left home, her quilting frame was always up in one of the empty bedrooms. She made quilts for each of her children and many of her grandchildren. In my earliest quilting memory, she is drafting a cable border on "my" quilt with a paper plate.

Fractal Man
80 x 60 inches, 1988
Anita Corum, Foresthill, California

Fractal, a geometric term, is a shape that looks more or less the same on any magnification of size or scale. Varying sizes of triangles are the fractal elements in this quilt. Rows of little men seen on the front and back complete the inspiration for the title.

A Place of My Own
39 x 58 inches, 1990
Cynthia England, Houston, Texas

A photograph, reminiscent of her grandfather's porch where
she played as a child, became the basis for this quilt. Another
view of the porch is seen in its mirror image on the back.

To England with Love
72 x 72 inches, 1990
Zena Thorpe, Chatsworth, California

Made as a love letter to England, the quilt's center panel has a crocheted lace border with the inscription, "There'll Always be an England." The Union Jack appears on both sides, while the bulldog carries the theme to the back.

Two Sides — One Idea

An idea or story expressed on the front can be extended to the back.
The theme can be portrayed by a simplified version of the front or
can further explain its meaning.

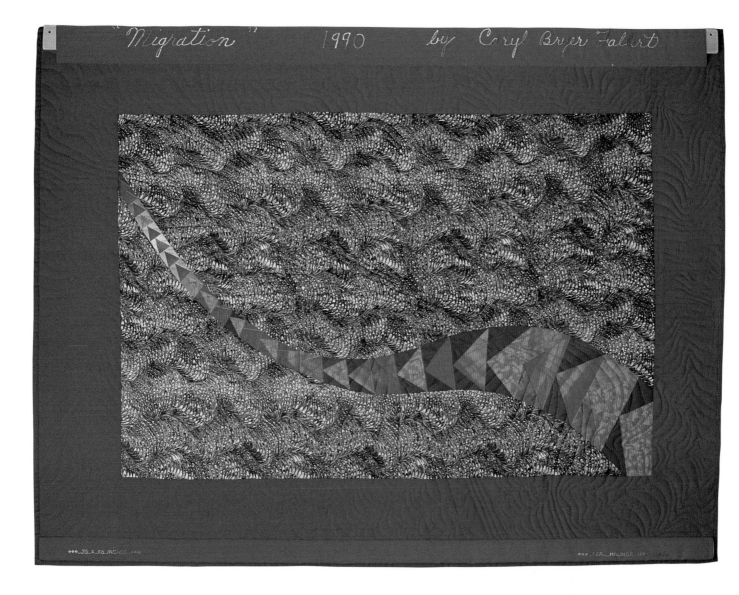

Migration
48 x 36 inches, 1990
Caryl Bryer Fallert, Oswego, Illinois
Collection of Malinda Jones, Clarindon Hills, Illinois

The maker likes to adapt traditional quilt patterns for the backs of her quilts as "a tribute to the creativity of the many anonymous quilt artists of the past." A variation of the traditional flying geese pattern reflects the front's theme of birds in flight.

Cosmic Connections
43.5 x 43.5 inches, 1991
Virginia King, Mountain View,
California

Nine repeated blocks depict the facade of organization vital to the maker. The metallic quilting visible on the back represents the energy that connects her to the cosmos.

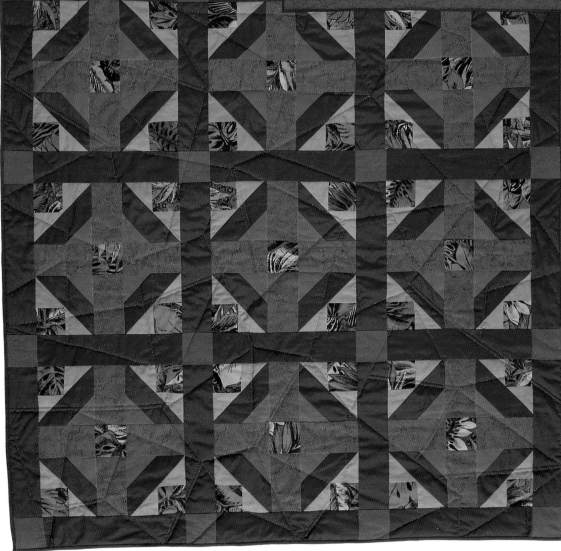

Chromatic Concerto
56 x 46 inches, 1989
Jean V. Johnson and Mary Gampper, Olathe, Kansas

Fifty-nine songs with names of colors in their titles are depicted on the front. The musical theme is carried to the back with the colorful band shell, the appropriate setting for a performance of the concerto.

Tiger, Tiger Burning Bright
45 x 54 inches, 1988
Yachi Nagamine Monarrez, Los Angeles, California

Appliques of printed tigers frolic through and about the
boxes on the quilt's front. Confetti, made from leftover bits
and pieces of fabric, tumbles out of a box on the back.

Black Mojave
88 x 99 inches, 1989
Vivian K. Choy, Lodi, California

At the quilt's top is a *noren* screen, a free-hanging curtain, depicting stars on the front and petroglyphs on the back. On the quilt's back, an appliqued scene represents the dawn of modern life. The snake signifies creation.

Emily
53 x 56 inches, 1990
Gail Garber, Rio Rancho,
New Mexico

In this quilt, inspired by quilter
Emily Bezzeg, an Indian girl is
seen against a landscape representing Shiprock, New Mexico,
a sacred place of the Indians.
On the back, the outline of the
girl's ghost appears in the night
sky above a row of mesas.

Pitcairn Island Quilt
75 x 84 inches, 1989
The people of Pitcairn Island and quilters from Hawaii
Coordinated by Rozemaryn van der Horst, Captain Cook, Hawaii

Commemorating the bicentennial of the arrival of the British ship, Bounty, and the landing of Fletcher Christian and the mutineers in 1790, this quilt was made to raise money for Pitcairn Island's school. In the detail of the back, a lone sailor represents Issac Martin, the only American mutineer. The pant flap folds down to reveal a label listing names of the participants.

You Can Always Count on a Scrappy
40 x 48 inches, 1989
Linda Graham, Los Angeles, California

The friendship blocks on the front were made by the
Scrappy Quilters of Los Angeles. The twelve participants
signed fabric squares that became the hand-shaped appliques
placed on the back behind their blocks.

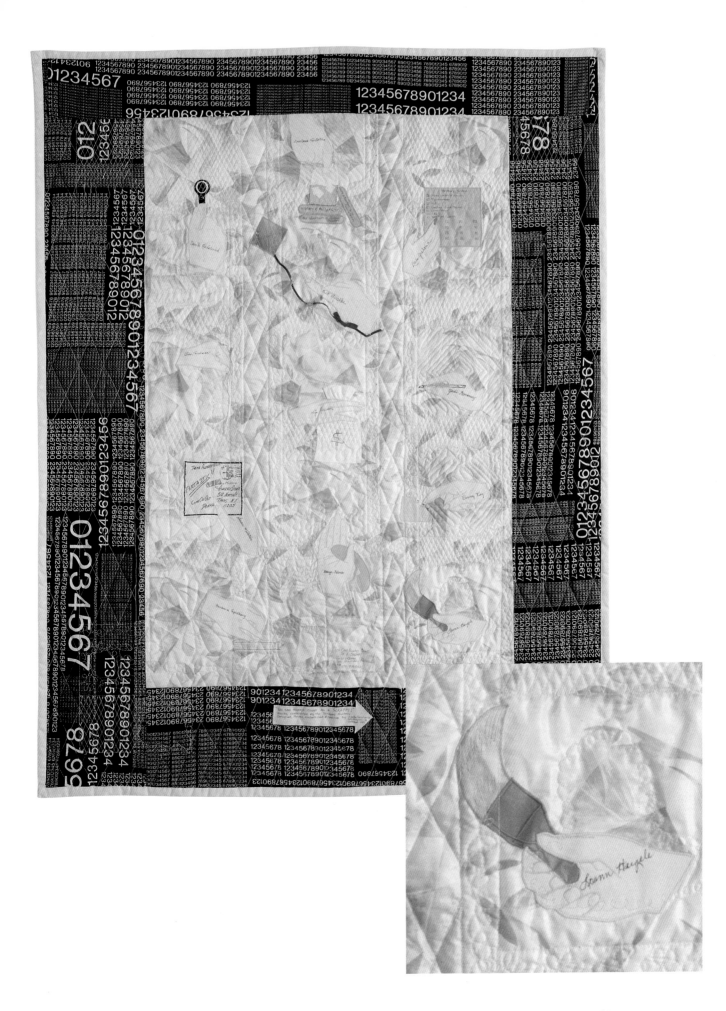

Bored Game
36 x 36 inches, 1989
Susan Galloway Wilson, Plano, Texas

This quilt is the result of the maker's frustration with the political power games played within her local quilt guild. Usually interesting women became as boring as the games they were playing. The backart reflects her strong feelings that a back is integral to an overall quilt design. She says, "I continue to involve the back of my quilts in the whole of my imagery."

70

Santa Fe: Sky Ceremony
48 x 37 inches, 1985
Judi Warren, Maumee, Ohio

In this contemporary quilt, the back becomes part of the front. The front reflects the colors of adobe walls and piñon trees. The back, folded to the front, represents the beautiful Southwestern sky.

Backart Techniques

The majority of quilt backs shown in this book were constructed using one or more of three techniques: horizontal/vertical cut, diagonal cut and framing. The techniques are described below in their simplest form. A variation is shown at the bottom of each page.

The following section contains information necessary to understand the three techniques. It should be read before beginning construction of a pieced back.

Basic Backart Guidelines

Determining the back's size. To guarantee that the back measures the size needed for the front, place the front on a large, flat surface such as the floor. It can also be taped on a wall. To gauge the size needed, leave the front in place, or mark its size on the surface with tape. While constructing the back, periodically compare its size to the size of the front.

Fabric insurance. When planning the back, always add an extra four inches beyond each side of the quilt front. This *insurance* guarantees that the back's final size will be larger than the front, allowing for easy alignment of the front and back.

Sewing the pieces. Sew the shortest seams together first. Sew straight edges to straight edges. Avoid inset piecing. Avoid placing bias edges on the outside edges of the quilt back.

Signing the quilt. A signature and date can be written using a permanent pen such as the Pilot SC-UF™ or the Pigma™ .01 and .05 in any color. A typed label is made by placing a light colored, prewashed fabric into a typewriter. Iron the fabric to set the ink. To test, write on a small piece of the fabric being used, then iron and wash the fabric.

Label: A piece of fabric containing the quilt's title and other pertinent information such as the maker and date.

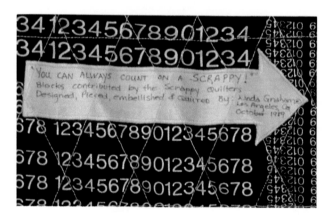

Detail of a handwritten label in Pigma™ ink from the back of "You Can Always Count On a Scrappy" page 68.

Horizontal/Vertical Cut

A simple horizontal/vertical back uses two lengths of fabric. One length is cut in half lengthwise and used for the outside columns. The second length becomes the center column. These fabrics can run either horizontally or vertically. Variations of this technique may be used to create fabric grids.

1. Measure the length and width of the quilt top. If the fabric selected for the back is as long as the quilt top, a vertical pieced back is recommended. If the fabric is too short *and* too narrow, consider a diagonal cut.

2. Cut the fabric along the center fold, producing two columns.

3. Place the two columns on the quilt top so that they extend beyond the top's edges by four inches on all sides. Measure the width of the space between the columns and cut another piece of fabric to that width including seam allowances.

——— pieces for back

- - - - - - quilt top

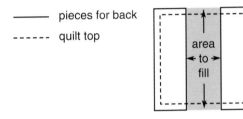

5. Sew the columns together.

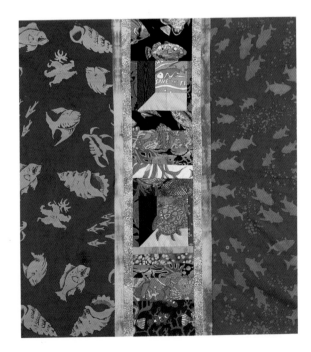

Variation: Columns can be pieced with leftovers from the front.

Leftovers: Blocks, strips or fabric intended for the front, but not used.

All the Fishes in the Sea
50 x 45 inches, 1991
Diana Leone, Santa Clara, California

Diagonal Cut

The diagonal cut utilizes fabric that is too narrow *and* too short to cover a quilt back. A larger piece of fabric may also be used. The basic diagonal cut uses two different pieces of fabric. One is cut on the bias, and the resulting triangles are placed at opposite corners of the quilt back. The second fabric is sewn between the two triangles. This technique is further explored in the section "Backs on a Slant."

1. Fold a piece of fabric from corner to corner, and cut along the fold. The fabric may be a square or a rectangle.

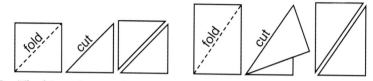

2. The bias edge can become wavy and stretch out of shape. To control this bias, sew a strip of fabric, cut on the straight of the grain, to each edge. The strips can be any width and should extend *beyond* the edges of each triangle. See variation below.

3. Place the two triangles on opposite corners of the top, overlapping its edges by four inches. Fill the area between the triangles with a piece of fabric. This piece must be long enough to extend *beyond* the corners of the front.

Do not trim the extra lengths of fabric. These *tails* will be trimmed after the quilt is layered.

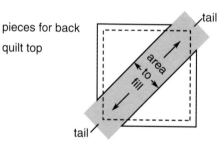

Variation: The middle panel can be pieced with leftovers from the front.

Birthday Quilt
65 x 65 inches, 1988
The Staff of Crazy Ladies and Friends,
Santa Monica, California
Collection of Kathryn Small

Framing

Framing may be used to showcase a special fabric. Simple frames can be created using the horizontal/vertical cut or the diagonal cut.

Horizontal/Vertical Frame. Sew strips of fabric to the top and bottom of the special fabric to form a central column. Sew columns of fabric to each side of the central column. These columns should be long enough to overlap the top's edges by four inches.

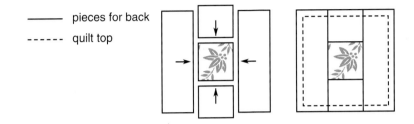

Diagonal Frame. Sew strips of fabric to the top and bottom of the special fabric to form a central column. This column must extend beyond the corners of the quilt's top. Proceed as in the diagonal cut instructions.

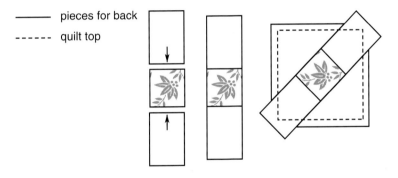

Variations: Sew multiple frames around a label.

Eat Your Veggies
30 x 30 inches, 1989
Danita Rafalovich, Los Angeles, California

75

Finishing Up

Most finishing processes are the same for quilts with backart and those with backs pieced from one fabric. Some differences occur with layering, quilting and sleeves. This section explains these differences.

For specific information needed to complete a quilt, refer to "Suggested Reading" for books that cover these subjects in detail.

Layering

Layering a quilt with backart is the same as for conventional backs, with a few exceptions. The batting selection is also the same as for conventional quilts.

The tails of a diagonal pieced back extend beyond the corners of the front. Trim these *after* the quilt has been layered and basted.

To accurately align seams on the back with seams on the front, place a pin straight down through all layers. Baste closer than usual, every two to three inches. This is an ambitious undertaking and not recommended for a beginner.

Quilting

A quilt with backart is basted and then hand or machine quilted in the same manner as a quilt with a conventional back.

Machine quilting: Since more than one fabric is used on the back, it is important to select a bobbin thread that best blends with all the fabrics. When working with multi-colored backs, gray is often the best color.

Hand quilting: In the case of multiple seams, use the stab stitch or slip the needle between the layers and leave a small area unquilted.

Sleeves

Sleeve construction is the same as for a conventional back when one fabric makes up the top five inches of the back. If these top five inches are pieced, we suggest piecing the sleeve to integrate it into the overall back design.

A pieced sleeve, as seen on Kathryn Pellman's quilt on page 28, is constructed out of two main parts — an outer portion that is pieced to match the design of the back and a lining portion made of one fabric. To create the sleeve "tube," sew the pieced front of the sleeve to the lining fabric (muslin, a solid colored fabric or fabric that matches the back). Whip stitch the top and bottom of the sleeve to the back.

Suggested Reading

Inspiration and Design Ideas

Crow, Nancy. *Nancy Crow: Quilts and Influences.* Paducah, KY: American Quilter's Society, 1990.

Porcella, Yvonne. *A Colorful Book.* Modesto, CA: Porcella Studios, 1986.

General Construction Techniques

Hopkins, Mary Ellen. *It's OK If You Sit on My Quilt Book.* Santa Monica, CA: ME Publications, 1989.

Horton, Roberta. *Calico and Beyond.* Lafayette, CA: C&T Publishing, 1985.

———. *Plaids & Stripes.* Lafayette, CA: C&T Publishing, 1990.

Leone, Diana. *The Sampler Quilt.* Mountain View CA: Leone Publications, 1986.

Mathieson, Judy. *Mariner's Compass.* Lafayette, CA: C&T Publishing, 1979.

McClun, Diana and Laura Nownes. *Quilts! Quilts!! Quilts!!!* Gualala, CA: The Quilt Digest Press, 1989.

———. *Quilts Galore.* Gualala, CA: The Quilt Digest Press, 1989.

Machine Quilting Techniques

Singer. *Quilting by Machine.* Minnetonka, MN: Cy DeCosse Incorporated, 1990.

Hargrave, Harriet. *Heirloom Machine Quilting.* Lafayette, CA: C&T Publishing, 1989.

Hand Quilting and Sleeve Application Techniques

Leone, Diana. *Fine Hand Quilting.* Mountain View, CA: Leone Publications, 1986.

Magazines

American Quilter. Paducah, KY: The American Quilters' Society.

Quilter's Newsletter Magazine. Wheatridge, CO: Leman Publications.

Quilting Today. New Milford, PA: Chitra Publications.

Index

About the Authors

Kathryn Alison Pellman and Danita Rafalovich met at a quilt guild meeting. Independently, they were experimenting with pieced quilt backs and decided to write their first article, "Backart — On the Flip Side," for *American Quilter* (Winter, 1988). They have award-winning quilts exhibited throughout the United States and are included in American and Japanese publications. Both have quilts in private collections. They each reside in Los Angeles, and both lecture and teach.

Kathryn has a Certificate in Fashion Design. Realizing she was no longer fulfilling her creative ambitions in the garment industry, she turned to quilting. Her work went full circle when she designed a quilted garment for Fairfield Processing's annual fashion show. Her current quilt series focuses on large one-frame stories or cartoon scenes expressing her opinions about society. She enjoys injecting a bit of humor into otherwise serious subjects.

Danita has a B.S. in Biology with an emphasis in Botany. She maintains extensive plant collections while her major focus of creativity is quilting. Currently, she is working on two series of quilts. One series is influenced by the year she spent living in Tokyo, Japan. The other is a humorous investigation of life illustrated with rubber stamp art. In addition, Danita teaches at Crazy Ladies and Friends, a quilt shop in Santa Monica, California.

Danita would like to thank her husband, Wayne Smith, for his generosity and consideration during the writing of this book.

For information about lectures and workshops given by Kathryn and Danita, write to

Danita Rafalovich
3956 Minerva Ave.
Los Angeles, CA 90066

Kathryn Alison Pellman   Danita Rafalovich

Other Leone Publications

The Sampler Quilt, Diana Leone	$11.95
Fine Hand Quilting, Diana Leone	$12.95
Quiltmaker's Book of 6" Patterns, Anthony & Lehman	$12.95
Attic Windows, Diana Leone	$14.95
Investments, Diana Leone	$14.95
Quiltmaker's Big Book of Grids, Anthony & Lehman	$14.95
Basic Seminole Patchwork, Cheryl Greider Bradkin	$16.95
Morning Star Quilts, Florence Pulford, soft cover	$24.95
Morning Star Quilts, hard cover collector's edition	$34.95

To order books:

Leone Publications, Dept. BA
2628 Bayshore Parkway
Mountain View, CA 94043

(415) 965-9797

For more information, send a self-addressed, stamped, legal size envelope.

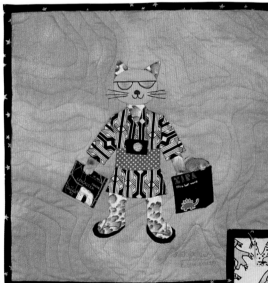

Kitty Quilter Goes to Japan
15 x 15 inches, 1989
Kathryn Alison Pellman, Los Angeles, California
Collection of Danita Rafalovich, Los Angeles, California

Utilizing Japanese prints, this quilt commemorates the year Danita lived in Tokyo, Japan. The framed airplane fabric became a label inscribed, "Kitty Quilter Goes to Japan — for Danita Rafalovich, world traveler."